SEVEN COLLAGES

HARRY CALLAHAN

ESSAY BY JULIAN COX

STEIDL

PACE / MACGILL GALLERY

1956/1957

Collage 1957

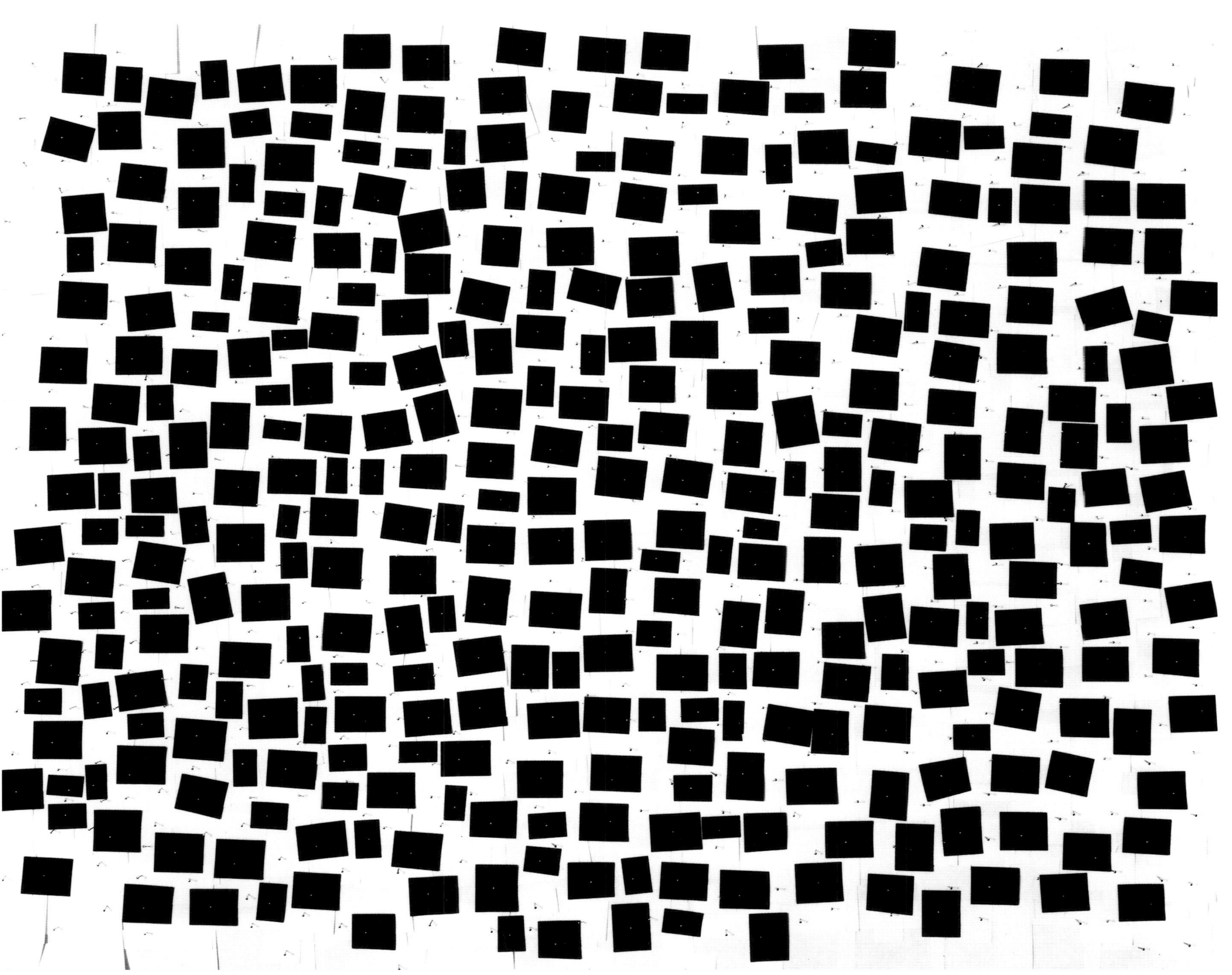

Collage 1957

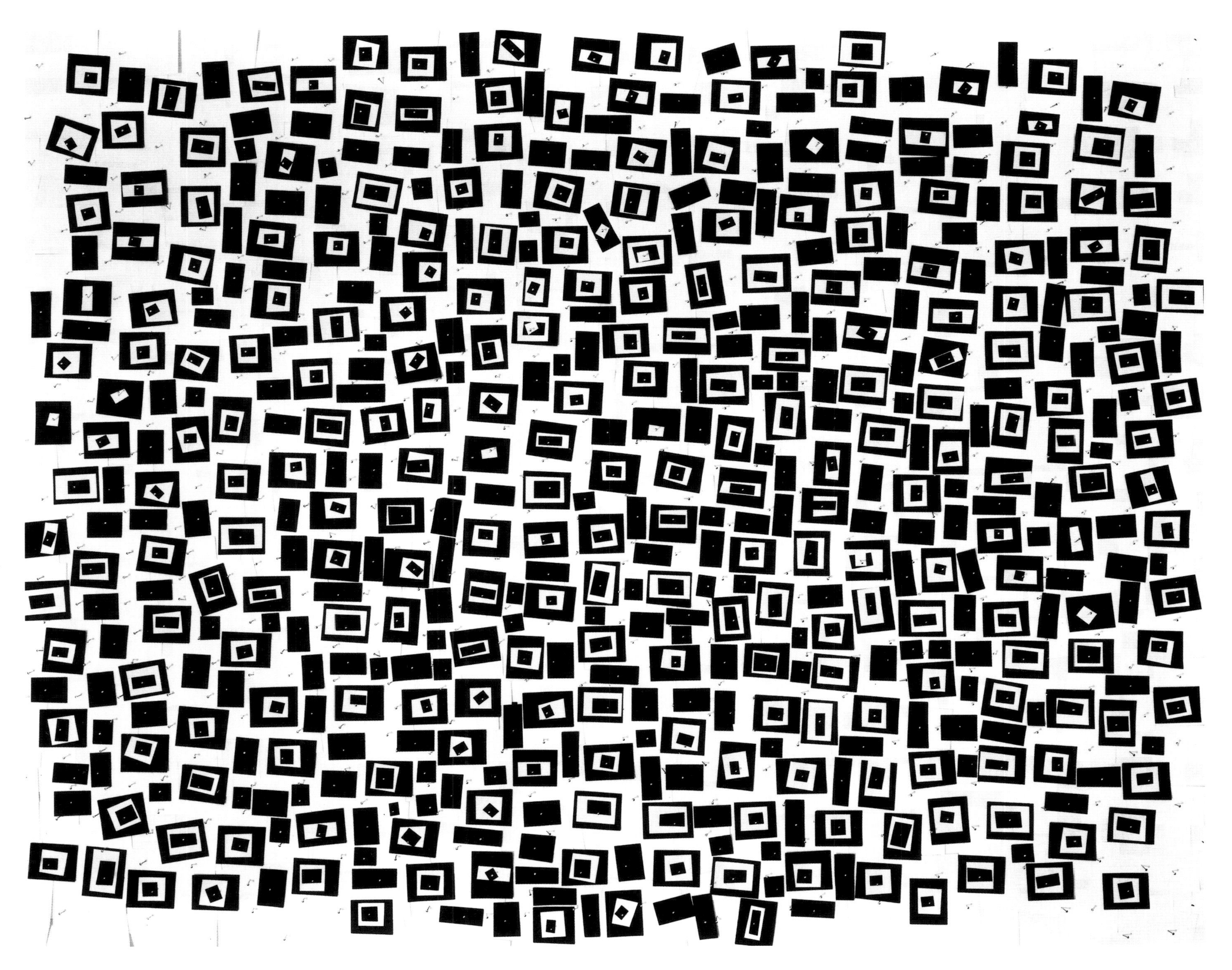

Collage 1957

Collage 1957

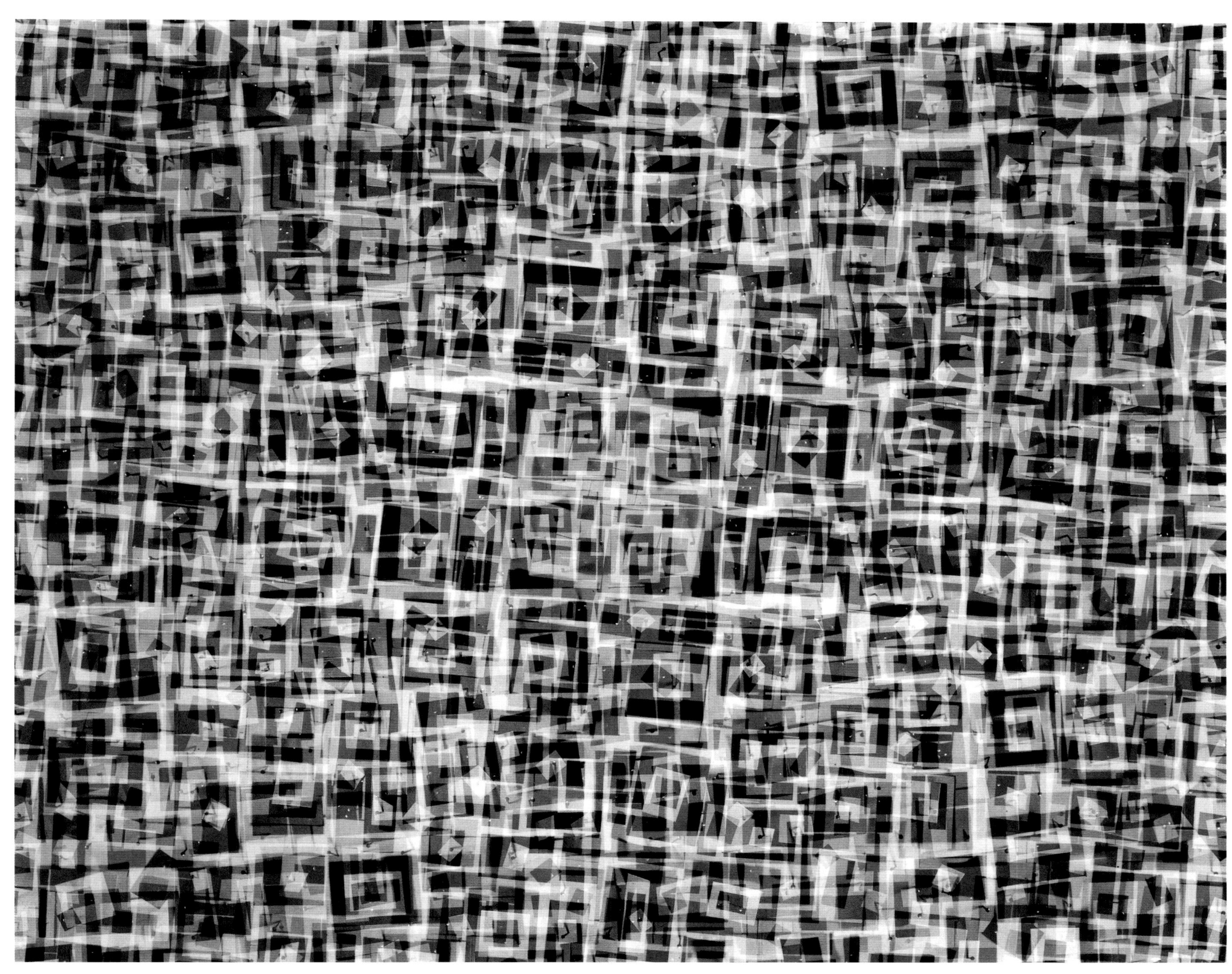

Collage 1956

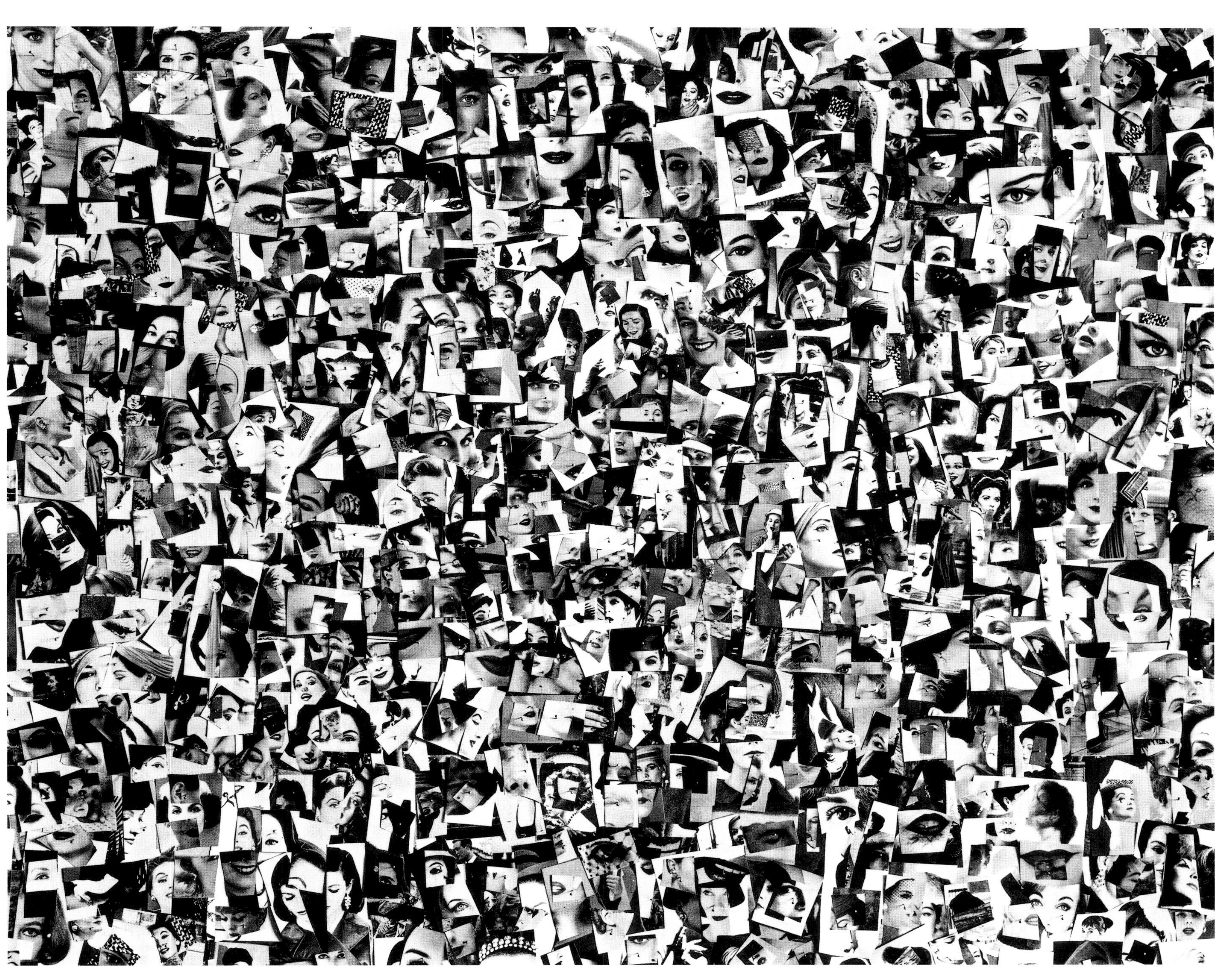

Collage 1956

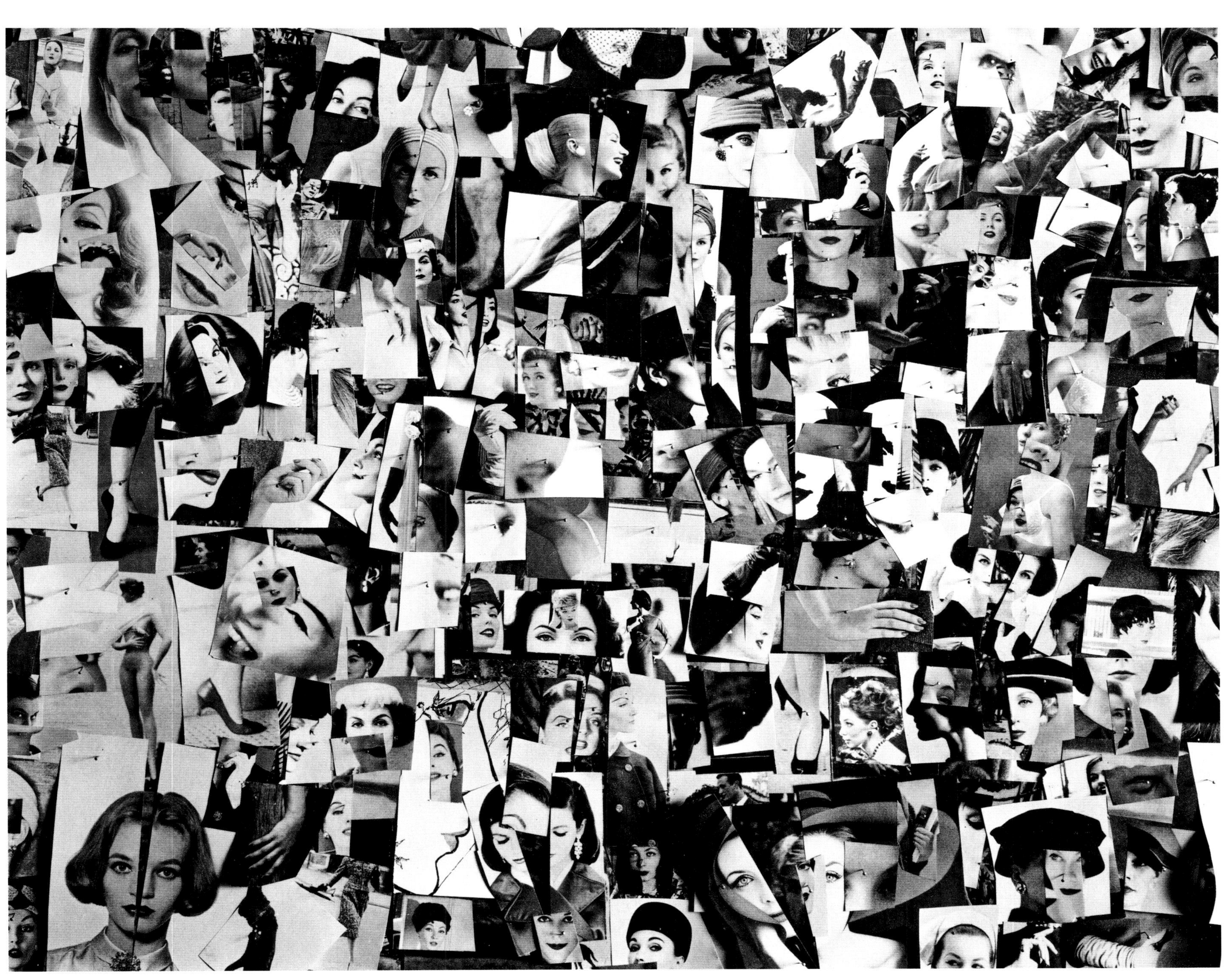

Collage 1956

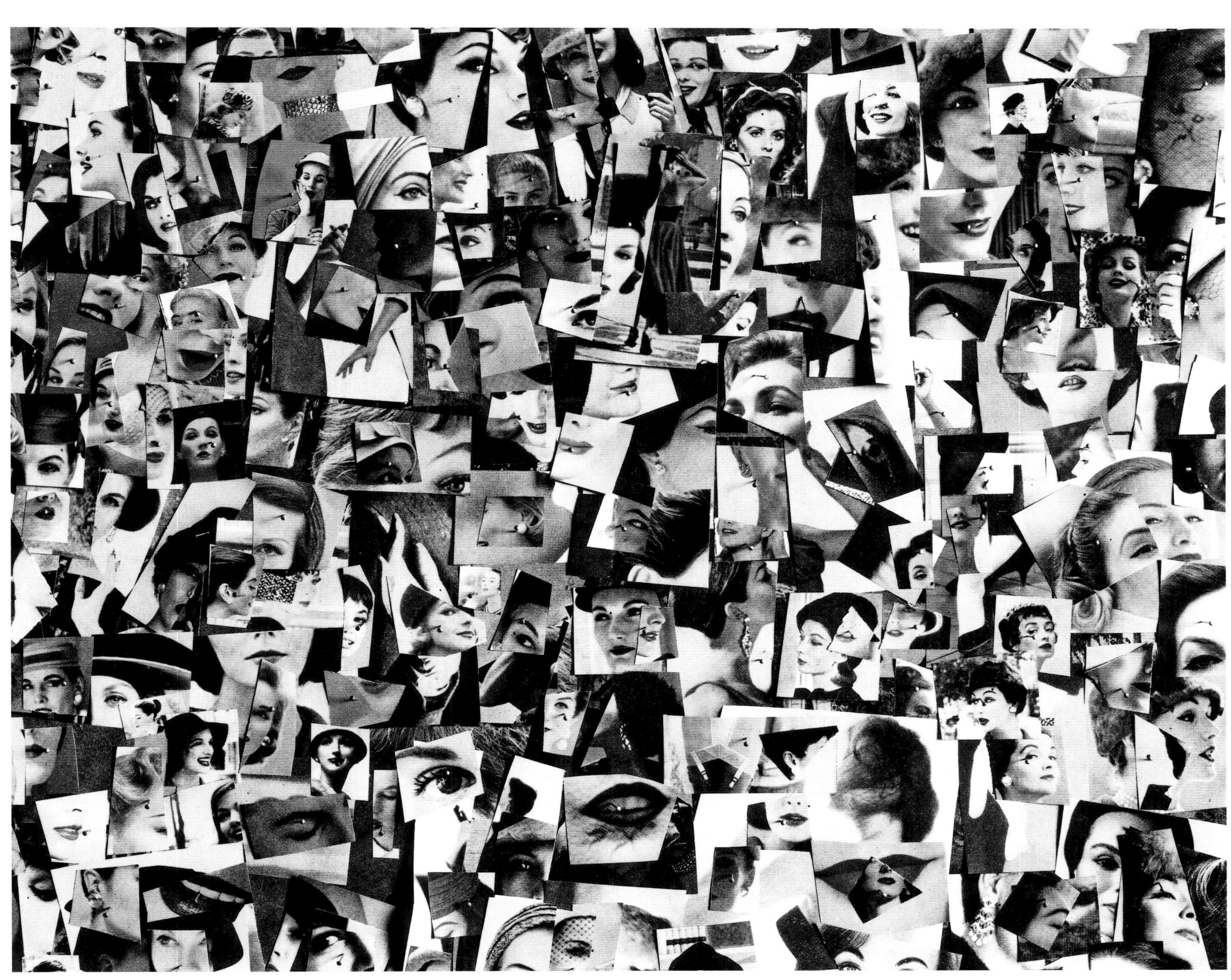

PROMISING MUTATIONS

To me the converging objects of the universe perpetually flow,
All are written to me, and I must get what the writing means.

Walt Whitman, *Leaves of Grass*

Harry Callahan was driven by a compulsion to know the world better by photographing it. The act of photographing—the process itself—was his primary concern and greatest delight. It allowed him to formulate a visual universe that gave meaning to his emotional life. Callahan was a man with a large desire for privacy, for whom photography was a safety net and the place to articulate some of his most intimate feelings. In 1946, in his first published declaration of an artistic philosophy, Callahan stated: "I am interested in relating the problems that affect me to some set of values that I am trying to establish as being my life. I want to discover and establish them through photography."[1]

Callahan came from the blue-collar suburbs of Detroit and a modest family where there was little interest in art or literature. He had to find his own path. Books provided access to a larger world, as did music and poetry, which became lifelong passions. Callahan enjoyed the classics of western literature, and was inclined towards poetry and prose that reflected the experiences of the regular, everyday person. He was impressed by the philosophical breadth and relentless, all-embracing energy of Walt Whitman's verse. The idea of personal freedom, and the example of fully developing one's potential with an attitude of emotional openness, freed him to find meaning in the world of familiar things. Throughout his long career Callahan intensively, almost obsessively, explored a relatively limited range of subjects—mainly architecture, nature, and street life, as well as his wife Eleanor and daughter Barbara (fig. 1)—but none of them is ever presented for psychological inquiry. It is the medium of photography that is repeatedly interrogated.

Achieving mastery over the expressive potential of his materials was key to Callahan's practice. He engaged tirelessly with formal and technical concerns, processing and printing his own black-and-white negatives and

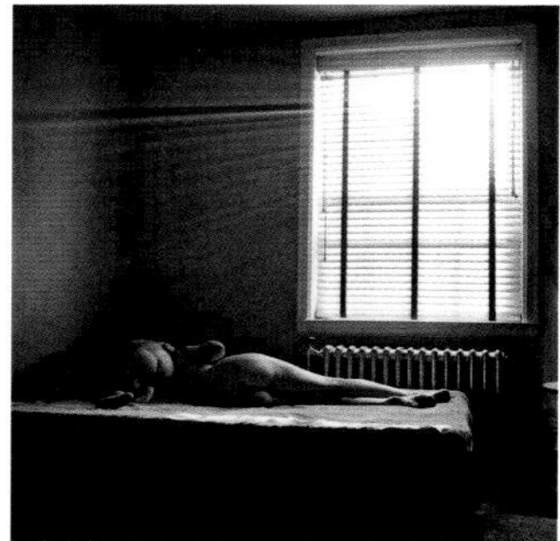

Fig. 1

photographing freely in all formats, from 35mm and medium format to 8 x 10 inch sheet film. He marveled at the possibilities that each apparatus allowed and the specific ways it pictured the world. Callahan's prolific productivity was such that the labor required simply to keep up with himself could at times become overwhelming.[2] His exacting approach to darkroom work goes back to his first encounter with Ansel Adams, who led a workshop at the Photographic Guild of Detroit in 1941.[3] Callahan drank deeply of the formalist doctrine of Adams, whose vision, sense of craft, and passion for the medium motivated him to work in his own way and to begin thinking of himself as an artist.

As early as 1942 Callahan had become adept at exposing film more than once in the camera, producing sophisticated overlays of complementary images. His skills in this arena and forays into related techniques were encouraged at the New Bauhaus in Chicago, established by the Hungarian émigré László Moholy-Nagy, who had taught at the original Bauhaus in Weimar, Germany, in the 1920s.[4] The curriculum entailed a steady flow of assignments that required experimentation in a variety of media and processes and the need for artists to fully comprehend the characteristics of their materials. Where photography was concerned this meant a repertoire that included unusual vantage points, multiple exposures, photograms, photomontage, color, and the concept of the photographic series, all of which were probed for their innate pictorial possibilities. The innovative spirit of the New Bauhaus agreed with Callahan's personality and his proclivity to establish meaning and understanding through process. He learned best through practice and by repeatedly engaging standard photographic problems. The self-imposed boundaries of controlled routine left him open to new ways of seeing. Callahan was not so interested in showing a logical or narrative progression between works. His curiosity led him to exploit the subtle variations that exist from image to image.

Callahan's aggressively modernist approach, and his will to methodically examine the possibilities inherent in a given motif or visual idea, are strongly in evidence in his collages of 1956-57. As with most of his series, Callahan established a set of parameters within which he could scrutinize and test specific effects, with an eye

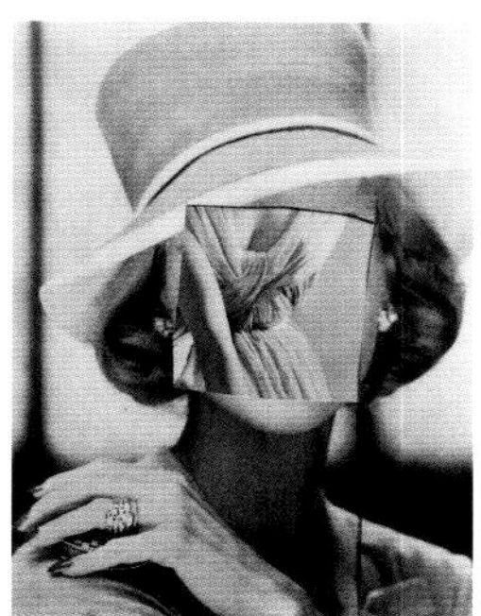

Fig. 2

to extending his photographic vocabulary into new territory. Of the seven collages in this book, three are assemblages of the truncated heads and body parts of female models cut from contemporary women's magazines. Callahan assembled them like jigsaw puzzles in his studio—discreetly varying the scale of the images in each composition—and then photographed the arrangement as a still life, with a tripod-mounted 8 x 10 inch camera. In the finished works, the actual physical edges of the collage are inconspicuous and the complex relationship of interlocking forms tends towards the surreal rather than the abstract. The remaining four collages consist of white on black, black on white sheets of paper that were pinned to a board in his studio and then photographed. The resulting images look like collage but are perhaps more accurately described as compositions of related objects clustered together in cell-like structures. Their delicious ambiguity is complicated (in two cases) by Callahan's deft use of multiple exposure, which radically alters the existing configurations of form and composition.

No curator better understood the pulse of Callahan's creative process than John Szarkowski, who once described the photographer's gift for what he called "the elastic ambivalence of photographic description."[5] This phrasing is particularly applicable to the collages, which are stripped of narrative insistence and provide no obvious entry points for exposition. They are playful, open-ended expressions of the fundamental plasticity of photography. A related set of pictures—made from the scraps of magazine cutouts (fig. 2)—underscores Callahan's restless inventiveness and readiness to strive for new understandings that might emerge from the rich intricacies of his visual imagination.

Although Callahan most likely would not have said as much, his desire to merge different visual and emotional worlds in his photography was part of a wider quest for a more open, accommodative kind of picture-making. The collages correspond to his belief that the flux and indeterminacy of the universe cannot necessarily be contained in a single, unadulterated image. In them he was able to dematerialize fixed notions of time and space, and reconfigure his "subject" in a new reality. He reveled in abandoning photography's traditional seamlessness in quest of the elusive and marginal terrains of photographic expression.

Julian Cox
Founding Curator of Photography and Chief Curator
Fine Arts Museums of San Francisco

[1] *Minicam Photography 9*, no. 6 (February 1946), 28-29.

[2] When Callahan's teaching commitments kept him from his regular darkroom routine, a backlog of unprinted negatives would result. The volume of unprinted negatives in the Callahan Archive at the Center for Creative Photography at the University of Arizona runs into several thousand.

[3] See Britt Salvesen, *Harry Callahan: Photographer at Work*, Tucson and New Haven: Center for Creative Photography and Yale University Press, 2006, 19-27.

[4] Ibid., 28-30. Callahan went on to teach at the New Bauhaus from 1946 to 1961. See also Charles Traub, ed., *The New Vision: Forty Years of Photography at the Institute of Design*, Millerton, New York: Aperture, 1982, unpaginated.

[5] John Szarkowski, *Callahan*, New York: Aperture/Museum of Modern Art, 1976, 21.

First edition published in 2012 / © 2012 Estate of Harry Callahan, collection of Caro Macdonald and Mark McCain/Eye and I for the images / © 2012 Steidl Publishers for this edition / All rights reserved. No part of this publication may be reproduced or transmitted in any form or by any means, electronic or mechanical, including photocopy, recording or any other storage and retrieval system, without prior permission in writing from the publisher. / Book design: Gerhard Steidl, Peter MacGill, and Duncan Whyte / Scans by Steidl's digital darkroom / Production and printing: Steidl, Göttingen / Steidl, Düstere Str. 4, 37073 Göttingen, Germany / Phone +49 551-49 60 60 Fax +49 551-49 60 649 / mail@steidl.de / www.steidlville.com / www.steidl.de / ISBN 978-3-86930-140-2 / Printed in Germany by Steidl